Animals in Fall

by Mari Schuh

Bullfrog
Books

Ideas for Parents and Teachers

Bullfrog Books let children practice reading informational text at the earliest reading levels. Repetition, familiar words, and photo labels support early readers.

Before Reading

• Discuss the cover photo. What does it tell them ?

• Look at the picture glossary together. Read and discuss the words.

Read the Book

• "Walk" through the book and look at the photos. Let the child ask questions. Point out the photo labels.

• Read the book to the child, or have him or her read independently.

After Reading

• Prompt the child to think more. Ask: What is fall like where you live? What do animals there do in fall?

Dedicated to St. Lucy Parish School of Racine, Wisconsin.

Bullfrog Books are published by Jump!
5357 Penn Avenue South
Minneapolis, MN 55419
www.jumplibrary.com

Library of Congress Cataloging-in-Publication Data
Schuh, Mari C., 1975-
  Animals in fall / by Mari Schuh.
    p. cm. — (Bullfrog books. What happens in fall?)
  Summary: "What do animals do in the fall to get ready for winter? Nature photographs and easy-to-read text tell kids how animals adapt to changing weather in the season of fall"— Provided by publisher.
  Audience: 005.
  Audience: K to grade 3.
  Includes bibliographical references and index.
  ISBN 978-1-62031-056-4 (hardcover : alk. paper) — ISBN 978-1-62496-074-1 (ebook)
  1. Animal behavior—Juvenile literature. 2. Autumn—Juvenile literature. I. Title.
  QL751.5.S38 2014
  591.5—dc23
                                    2013001946

Series Editor: Rebecca Glaser
Series Designer: Ellen Huber
Photo Researcher: Heather Dreisbach

Photo Credits:
Alamy, 16; Biosphoto, 20–21; Dreamstime, 8-9, 11, 15, 22tl, 22bl, 22tr, 22br, 23bl, 23mr; Getty, 4, 7; Shutterstock, cover, 1, 3t, 3b, 5, 6, 10, 12, 13, 14, 17, 23tl, 23ml, 23tr, 23br, 24; Superstock, 18-19

Printed in the United States of America at Corporate Graphics, in North Mankato, Minnesota.
5-2013 / PO 1003
10 9 8 7 6 5 4 3 2 1

Table of Contents

Busy Animals

Fall is here.

**Animals are busy.
They are getting ready
for cold weather.**

Squirrels bury nuts.

They will eat
them later.

7

Geese migrate.
They fly south.

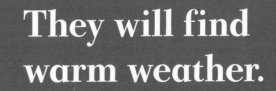

They will find warm weather.

Bats hide in a cave.
They will sleep
all winter.

cave

Black bears eat more food in the fall.

They will sleep in their dens.

Foxes grow thick fur.

The fur will keep them warm.

Snowshoe hares
change colors.

Their white fur will
match the snow.

Ladybugs look for a safe home.
They will hide in logs.

Some will hide
under rocks.

The animals
are ready.

Cold days will
come soon.

A Snowshoe Hare Changes

fall

winter

summer

spring

Picture Glossary

bury
To hide something by putting it in the ground and then covering it.

hare
An animal that is much like a rabbit, but a little larger.

cave
A large, hollow space in the ground.

migrate
To move from one area to another when the seasons change.

den
An animal's home; animals make dens in burrows, caves, under rocks, and in tree holes.

weather
What the outside air is like at a certain time and place.

Index

To Learn More

Learning more is as easy as 1, 2, 3.

1) Go to www.factsurfer.com

2) Enter "animalsinfall" into the search box.

3) Click the "Surf" button to see a list of websites.

With factsurfer.com, finding more information is just a click away.